Potent Poems for Pedagogues

Potent Poems for Pole-Axed Pedagogues

Mike Kivi
with illustrations by Bill Stott

Trentham Books

First published in 1992 by Trentham Books Limited

Trentham Books Limited
Westview House
734 London Road
Oakhill, Stoke-on-Trent
England ST4 5NP

British Library Cataloguing in Publication Data
Kivi, Mike
    Potent Poems for Pole-Axed Pedagogues
    I. Title
    821.914

    ISBN: 0 948080 71 X

Acknowledgments
Grateful thanks to *Education* magazine, *The Times Educational
Supplement* and many other journals where the works in this
volume were first published.

Designed and typeset by Trentham Print Design, Chester and
printed in Great Britain by BPCC Wheatons Limited, Exeter.

For Virginia

Contents

Foreword

George Low

'You can't speak to Mr Kivi — he's teaching' was the way the author of this slim volume swam into my ken. A mysterious letter had arrived with some highly original and amusing verses attached and it seemed only natural (and even irresistible) to follow up the letter with a phone call.

Who was this teacher from somewhere in Cheshire who could turn his hand to so many pastiches and parodies at the drop of a hat? Was Kivi perhaps a subtle pseudonym for some satirist in high places bent on ridiculing the absurdities of our educational masters?

In due course Mike Kivi phoned back — at break time. The bustle and echoes on the corridors could be heard in the background. Yes, he'd be delighted to tidy up the poem (he would do that in his lunch break, he explained) and it would be in the post on his way back from school. The ERA Express arrived the next day and its scurrying stanzas 'This is the nightmare bringing the orders, Out of the capital up to the borders...' have now been reprinted in teachers' publications all over the kingdom.

After that a steady flow of verse came down on the night trains from Crewe to *Education* — each one more original than the last. Not only could Mike Kivi write when the mood took him, he could even perform to order. It is almost unknown, at least since the days of Homer, for a contributor to offer an epic poem as a news report. But that iş what Mr Kivi came up with on the National Union of Teachers' special salaries conference at Scarborough two years ago (see *The Scarborough Tales* in this volume).

In Bill Stott, the poet has his perfect illustrator — a cartoonist with the same pungent humour and freshness of style. Also from the North-West, Bill Stott shares the gallowsbird outlook of the ordinary classroom teacher — condemned to suffer the slings and arrows of Ministers and politicians, the avalanche of Government regulations, the latest theories of advisers, the rare sightings of HMI, the edicts of heads and the unpredictabilities of governors.

The combination of the two will bring a tonic of light relief to the teacher's day and will be read, reread and memorized in staffrooms and classrooms throughout the land.... from Somerset to Fakenham, from Carlisle to Kirklees.

"Change is not made without inconvenience..."
—Dr Johnson

The ERA Express

This is the nightmare bringing the orders
Out of the capital up to the borders;
Orders for governors, orders for heads,
Making them turn in their uneasy beds,
Worrying little ones still in their prime,
And teachers who cannot deliver on time,
Covering desk tops with binders and folders,
Weighing them down like enormous grey boulders,
Whistling through dreams like a demon that rages,
Hurtling along on its iron key stages.
This is the nightmare slowly ascending,
Mountains of paperwork, tests never ending;
Ranks of advisers all on the offensive,
From nursery corner to state comprehensive,
Throwing out history books, tearing up parchments,
Re-educating the heads of departments,
Casting a searchlight on matters curricular,
Auditing every classroom particular,
Hurtling through concepts regardless of stress,
Racing to get there before LMS,
Puffing and straining at terrible pace,
Sweating to put all the targets in place,
Until it arrives at its last destination,
The terminal scrapyard of state education.
Out of the capital, over the borders,
This is the nightmare bringing the orders,
The cold steel of audit, assessment and test,
Laying democracy surely to rest.

Caught in the Act

They're sitting them in Somerset,
They're doing them in Devon,
They're taking them in Fakenham,
Performing them in Nevin.
From Carlisle down to Kettering
They're struggling at their best
In vain attempts at bettering
Each other in their tests
They're taking trials in Sunderland,
Lamenting them in Leeds,
For some it's just a wonderland
(like those with special needs).
They're scathing up in Scarborough,
Complaining in Kirklees,
While down in Market Harborough
They're falling on their knees.
They're plagued with pique in Pontefract,
Despite the licquorice fields,
And Durham's dizzy with the Act
From Stockton to South Shields.

In every school in every town,
Assessment is the word,
And every child's a helpless clown
Performing the absurd.
If seven seers spent seven years
In transcendental bliss,
They'd never dream an astral scheme
As lunatic as this.

Now We are Theven

If I can read a hundred wordth,
If I can do my betht,
And if my lithp ith not abthurd
When I perform my tetht...
And if I can rehearthe my book
Before my firtht exam,
Then maybe Nanny Clarke will cook
Thome buttered thconeth and jam.
And if I don't make one mithtake
And gain a thtandard three,
Perhapth there'll be thome fairy cake
For Nanny Clarke and me!

Now We are Theven (PE)

I'm planning my performantheth
For drama and PE,
I think I'll choothe the beanbagth
And the ballth from clathroom three,
Perhapth I'll pick the Murphy twinth
To join my danthe formation,
They're good in clath performantheth
And love partithipation.
I'm going to bounthe a tennith ball
Around Mith Taylorth bin,
And if I do it thkilfully
Thith time it might go in,
And Jamie Murphyth very good
At throwing thingth around —
I hope that I can catch them all
Before they hit the ground.
My teacher thayth I've got to jump
And hold my feet apart,
But Jamie thayth it'th quite alright
To thimply make a thtart.
To tell the truth, I don't feel well,
I feel an awful meth,
And jumping while I'm chattering
Jutht taketh away my breath —
And often I get very hot,
My fathe becometh all red.
I hope they thtop thith tethting thoon
Tho I can go to bed.

Now We are Theven (Muthic)

I really love my muthic clath
We have it in the hall,
The nithetht thing about it ith
There are no boyth at all.
I don't like drumth or bagpipeth,
I think they're far too loud —
I'm really betht at thinging
Ethpethially to a crowd.

My teacher liketh my thinging voithe,
She thayth I'm trying hard,
Exthept thometimeth she maketh me go
To practithe in the yard.
I find thome wordth quite difficult,
Like largo and vibrato —
And I don't know why she'th chrithtened me
A little othtinato.

Hunting Song for the New Year

Do ye ken Ken Clarke at the break of year
With a voice that is oiled on traditional beer,
And a message that every teacher will fear
As he shouts out his plans of appraisal.

Oh, the sound of his voice and the things he said
(And the thoughts of the empty hospital bed)
Could just be the thing to kill teaching dead
As he sings out his songs of appraisal.

Do ye ken Ken Clarke at the break of day
Do ye ken Ken Clarke in his suit of grey
With a package to frighten new teachers away
As he lays down the laws of appraisal.

Do ye ken Ken Clarke with his new suede shoes
His taste for jazz and traditional booze,
It's no wonder that teachers are singing the blues
As he stamps out the beat of appraisal.

Oh, the noise he makes and his awful shout,
The hint of a sneer and his schoolboy pout
Could easily bring the whole workforce out
As he drives them to heartless appraisal.

18

New Year's Briefing

And who are these constrained and careworn creatures,
Within the twilight of a darkened room,
Anxiety the hallmark of their features,
Foreboding heavy in the silent gloom?

These are the ones whose souls the system savaged,
Whose memories bear the scars of battles lost;
These are the ones that testing times have ravaged —
Who gave their all and did not count the cost.

Now they return with dull anticipation,
A spiritual bond their one remaining strength,
To hear again the New Year's exhortation
Repeated but at so much greater length.

"We must work harder, stretch our slim resources,
We must beware the loony liberal call,
Come let us praise the power of fiscal forces...
A happy market year to one and all!"

The Clarke Rising

Busie old Clarke, unruly Ken
Why dost thou thus
Through noysie presse releeses call on us?
Can teachers ever know the moment when
Some new instructionne or lore
May fall withinne directed tyme —
Or when the insubstantial staffroom dore
Shall tremble to new legislationes ryme,
The harbinger of yet another box
Repleet with ordres welcome as the pockes.

I wonder by my troth how infantes did
Until we met
Continue in theyre alphabet
Or lerned (without assessmentes parfait grid)
To rede and write, to daunce and singe
To play with balls, to swimme and runne,
To lerne the joyes of daffodils in springe,
Or even rede the poesye of Donne?
Were wee, until this moment, in the darke,
Cast only in the role of simple clerke?

Thy wordes so confident and full of strengthe
Bewilder us;
For though they speke full volume and at lengthe
Of rapid change in everye syllabus,
Thy reverie of state controules
Casts feare on those in littel schooles
Who strive to kepe from harm the tendre soules
Of children used as market fortune's fooles.
Remember ye, who turn the worlde to testes,
Who orders motion seldom ever restes!

"HUH! YOU WON'T FIND ANY INSPECTOR CATCHING ME NAPPING, I CAN TELL YOU... WHAT'S THAT FUNNY LITTLE BOX THING SOMEBODY'S SCREWED TO THE WALL?"

A table for our times

Two ones are two,
Two twos are four,
Here's the inspector
Coming through the door.
One three is three,
Two threes are six,
Cover up the sand tray,
Throw away the bricks.

One four is four,
Two fours are eight,
Sit down and shut your mouth,
How dare you lose your slate!
One five is five,
Two fives are ten,
This scribble's far too small,
Dot it all again!
Put away the paintpots,
Finish off those sums,
Get down to your phonic work,
Sit down on your bums!

Here is the inspector,
You all know what to do,
He used to check the water mains —
Now he's checking you!
We've paid a lot of money
So we'll have a good report,
It isn't very funny,
So show him how you're taught!

Two threes are six,
Three threes are nine,
Here's the inspector
Coming down the line.
Time to get your pencil out
And throw away your blocks,
Now copy out this cursive script,
PULL UP YOUR TINY SOCKS!

On Spellynge

Had we but world enough and time
This critick voys woyld be no crime,
Such sawcy words would fill the houres
With merrynesse like scented floures.

But at my back I hear the knell
Of antique linguist Fred Schonell,
Whose list of spellynges good and true
(Macmillan, 1932)
Referred to coyly now and thenne
Has crauled back into vogue agen.

Once more our toil is press'd with feares
Of sleeplesse nights and infant teares.
And with what toil we fill our day!
Whose houres are long but flie away,
While concepts trickle thorough the classe
Like graines of sand within a glas.

O, must we now with phonic crie
Assault the TV tutor'd eye
With lerning of each graded stage
Up to the final fiftieth page?

No, rather taste a serpente's stinge
Or teach a mermaid how to singe,
Than smite a childe with errour's rod
And terror of the Morphic god...
For transient are infant joys
When magick dreames are broke by noyse,
And tales coelestiall, heav'n made,
Returned corrected, with a grade.

"YES WE HAVE LEARNED FROM OUR FAILURES..."

Old Major's Dream

My friends, I had a dream last night
Of magic force and power
A dream that cast a burning light
In Monmouth's darkest hour
And in this dream did noble Ken
A new estate decree,
Where young and old, both maids and men
Receive their own degree.
So here is my election call,
A promise for all classes,
A new diploma free for all
And vouchers for the masses —
Certificates for architects,
For gardeners in parks,
For poets, vets and programmers
For painters and for clerks,
Diplomas for the legal types
Preparing for the bench,
Certificates for labourers
And professeurs of French,
For managers in factories
For workers down on farms
For captains and for colonels
And corporals at arms.
Diplomas to the left of them,
Diplomas to the right
The educated unemployed
Will march into the night.

The Great Debate

Now is the spring of bitter discontent
Made humourous by the naughty Prince of Wales,
And shadowy experts, filled with foul intent
Protest the virtue of their sacred grails;
While sober politicians nod their heads
In part agreement with the Prince's words,
Protest the schools are occupied by reds
Who sow the seeds of young rebellious herds.
They curse the hidden social engineers
Who plan their days with anarchic intrigue,
But disagree with baseless royal fears
That innovation causes much fatigue.
Around the forum angry voices cry,
The speech is heated, vacuously debated;
The noble Prince will surely breathe a sigh,
At nonsense that is so unmitigated.
Now entertain this lecture for our time,
This brave attack on cultural demise,
On literacy and lack of classic rhyme,
And absence of dear Shakespeare's glittering prize,
This bold aside to clerks and men of straw —
Mark well and act on what your Prince has said:
Give more to the ones who teach, dear friends, much more,
Or call the soul of English teaching dead.

In Loco Majoris

Now contemplate this strange election rhyme,
Created in the absence of a muse
To fill the mists of parliamentary time
With secret whispers kindled to confuse:
Bold words of fire light up the cloistered dark
To stir the tardy-gaited Kinnock horde
As, smiling, noble Kenneth Harry Clarke
Assumes the mantle of the self-assured.
Atop the hill a purple banner flies,
Its message evanescent in the gloom,
While old Jack Straw with sanctimonious sighs,
Condemns the weary path of Chartist doom.
Now Kenneth Harry (Glory on his head)
Goes forth to brave the wave of media scorn,
His largesse universal, overfed
With rhetoric and old infertile corn.
Upon his face there is no note of fear,
His liberal eye presents a harmless gaze;
And, soft, there is a sympathetic tear ...
He comes to make them merry, not appraise.
His words bring comfort to the poor condemned,
Beset by foul political intrigue,
As, confident, he rushes to commend
The virtues of the Royal Premier League.
"This is no test of mettle, gentle knights,
Mark well my promise, heed the words I say,
For bountiful will be the fiscal rights
Of those who fight upon election day!"
And, thus, he leaves them staring each to each,
To entertain the portents of the fight,
A paragon for all who feign would teach,
A little touch of Harry in the night.

Electoral Pectoral

Roll up lads, roll up lasses,
Don't forget yer tinted glasses!
Get yer shining charter here,
No smokescreen, no cheap veneer.
No more esoteric prose,
Not one sniff of emperor's clothes!
Come and try this startling bargain,
Free from circumventive jargon.
Read this new and wondrous fable,
Scan the great performance table!
Board the bureaucratic barque,
Roll up for yer Chartermark!
Buy this thrilling lista nova —
Just three million copies over!
Come on kiddies, step inside,
Bring yer parents on the ride,
Grab this final chance to barter,
Come on suckers, get yer charter!

Jack's Pact

I pledge to keep my children neat,
To make their rosy faces glow,
To buy new school shoes for their feet,
And curb their use of video.
I undertake that I will keep
An interest in their games and sport,
To put them early down to sleep
And check their skirts are not too short.
I vouch to buy their PE kit,
A pencil and a metric rule,
And swear that they will be equipped
With proper attitudes to school.
I covenant that every year
I'll buy them books at Christmas time,
And make it absolutely clear
That watching Neighbours is a crime.
I give my word that I will go
To every consultation night,
That everyone in school will know
If things at home are not quite right.
But why, I ask, this martyred smile,
Why do they trudge to school so slow;
Resenting every chartered mile,
Miles of sadness, miles of woe?

The Adviser's Curriculum Vitae

I am the new administrator found across the nation
I've given the establishment a new interpretation
I easily combine the roles of officer/adviser
And in the field of management there is nobody wiser.

I am a most enlightened man, but never talk of manning;
I think in terms of services and strategy and planning.
My mind is fixed on absolutes, there's nothing left to chance;
I never work with structures that depend on clrcumstance.

My clients know they can rely upon my firm assurance,
And my establishment support has guaranteed endurance.
I help my schools to understand from general to particular
Such esoteric concepts as 'cross-phase' and 'cross-curricular'.

I'm readily quite capable of praising heads with unction,
(But let them take great care who don't perform their proper function)
My protocol is measured to the very smallest fraction
And I am always ready to employ corrective action.

I know there are as many styles as there are LEAs
But my adaptability will frequently amaze.
I often change from officer, to deputy, to chief —
Mercurial ability that's quite beyond belief.

I am the new administrator found across the nation;
Well versed in matching task and role, and cost evaluation.
I'm easily quite capable of wearing Emperor's clothes
In fact I'll do most *anything* to please my CEOs.

* Chief Education Officers

The Students' Friend's Tale

I know a bank where every student goes
To seek the means of warmth, and food, and clothes,
And where, within the secret of its trees,
Lies wealth enough to pay tuition fees.
There once were many banks with such resources
Until they saw the absence of black horses,
And as the loan scheme prospects ceased to glisten,
Those other banks began to think and listen.
Now there remains one governmental place
Where students may present their lowly case,
To borrow wealth and beg for sustentation,
That they may eat while in their education.
There could be problems paying back the loans,
But proctors can record what each one owns,
And if a student does not prove his worth,
Right soon I'll put a girdle round this earth.
I'll follow him from sunset until day
To take my due from his postgraduate pay.
Agreed, this won't replace the student grant,
But let us not indulge in wingeing cant —
For there will be no adverse cashflow hitch
For those whose parents are well heeled or rich.
These loans will be a blessing for the poor,
Who'll find each polytech an open door.
Yes, there's a bank that every student knows,
Where interest like luscious woodbine grows,
Where all receive a worthless plastic card
And words of promise worthy of a bard.

... of Persons and Angels

There's nice it is in Dylan's dingle
Deep in darkest Wales,
There's lovely swapping half bilingual
Juicy Celtic tales;
There's smashing reading metaphysics
Rich in ancient power,
There's magical the mystic lyrics
Told of Old Glendower.

There's super sailing surfing bays
With Mary and Myfanwy,
Those Welsh and wonderous holidays
In Criccieth and Deganwy.
There's lovely reading Whitehall's rules
In Gwalia's gorgeous tongue,
And hearing heavenly harps in schools
Where old Welsh songs are sung.

There's brave of England's government,
There's ethnically aware.
Let's hope that's not its full extent,
Let's hope they don't stop there.
There's just a slight perversity
Which might stir ethnic anger:
For linguistic diversity
Does not quite end in Bangor...

A Language for Life

Deep in the shadiest mists of infant time
Exists a faerie dream of summer's day,
Where kindly heads consider it a crime
To disallow appeals for longer play;
Where flowers are plucked to touch, to smell, to dream,
Not tabulated on some mystic chart,
Where joy, not cold assessment is the scheme,
And tranquil patience calms the teacher's art.
True pastorale is nursed in every school,
While Nature's order creeps in day by day,
And gentle reason is the only rule
Upon those lost idyllic fields of play.
Such fields are measured, charted and portrayed,
Expressed in colour, formed in simple rhyme,
And lovingly these labours are displayed
In thoughtful friezes, tapestries sublime.
Such dreams are gone, and words can not recall
Those moments free from bureaucratic strife;
Now language serves no fruitful use at all
And minutes are for meetings, not for life.

Funding Fate

Mrs Dover drives her Rover
Through the gaily streamered gate,
Banners flying boldly over,
Welcome to our Summer Fête.

Through the car park lined with prefects,
Past the painted cycle shed,
(Blotting out its timber defects)
To the *Space Reserved For Head.*

In the classroom first year pupils
Revel in a retail heaven,
Advertising without scruple
Crafty Bargains by Year Seven

Girls in frilly caps and aprons
Carry coffee on a tray,
Cuffs and collars cut from paper
Given by the PTA.

In the playground Mrs Rickett
Sits upon a wooden stool
Only twenty pence a ticket:
Duck a Teacher in the Pool!

Far across the hockey pitches
Stands a clutch of deputies
Gowned like medieval witches
Beneath the well established trees.

Round their feet in form most frightful
Sheets of latex wreathed in death,
Much more evil than delightful,
A bouncy beast devoid of breath.

Sixth form girls are getting ready
Setting up their fancy stalls:
Guess my Weight and *Name the Teddy,*
Shoot the Table Tennis Balls!

Fifth year leavers sneer and, glaring,
Smoke their brazen cigarettes,
Ghetto blasters loudly blaring
Heavy acid rock cassettes.

Mrs Cato sells potatoes
In Elizabethan smock,
In the gym Miss Nimble capers
Shameless in a mini-frock.

Now the cash is flowing freely,
Kisses Free with each Balloon,
Watch your teacher do a Wheelie!
Kids v Staff — this Afternoon.

Gathered in their shorts and Reeboks,
Teachers show their hairy thighs,
Girls in boots and dirty kneesocks
Giggle with mischievous eyes.

Children cheer and shout for action,
Caring less which team might win,
The head of art, with satisfaction,
Kicks a governor on the shin.

Fast the fevered game progresses,
Accusations grow more brash,
First years pick up creamy messes,
Clerks and typists count the cash.

Mr Bullock from the county
Makes the draw for all the prizes,
Whisky, wine and smaller bounty,
Down to very tiny sizes.

Rover filled with surplus flowers,
Mrs Dover drives to town,
The stress of long but happy hours
Producing just a little frown.

35

On the bypass round the city
Mrs Dover, apprehensive,
Avoids a building grey and gritty,
The sinking downtown comprehensive.

A sign disturbs her calm composure,
Above the old Victorian gate:
These premises are due for closure.
A melancholy summer fate.

The Detailed Provisionnes — A Songe for Halloween

Now is the magick season come arounde
Whenne innocentes must studie light and sounde,
Must daunce like spirits in a faerie ring
To perce the roote of everich living thing,
Now, seated in the drede enchaunted chayre
It is the time to weigh the rockes, the ayre,
To find the mystick properties of fyres
Beset by bulbes and straunge magnetick wyres.

Now taste the crust of stayle curricular brede
And mesure sonnesettes shades of redde,
While infantes watch the flecked derke of night
In serche of morweninges hopefulle streak of light,
As balefulliche hem trudge the felde and ponde
Within a wery tredmill of disponde.

Make thick the gruwell of water, wax and ice,
Dissolve, and squash, and pour to make it nyce,
Now bend and twist the wood into the soyle,
Then bring the sweltered venom to the boyle.
Take hemlock roote well hidden from the day
To analyse its natural decay.

Regard with critick eye the weatheres mood,
See how it chaunges plastick, waste and food;
Now plucke and blowe, then stretch and shake and scrape,
Marke well the magick compostes aweful shape.
Mix in the sewage, sand, more soyle and rockes,
Watch well the rippling wayves in springes and lockes.
Softe, here the echo in the moonelit skie:
The owlet screech, its floatinge, synkinge crie.

Now harness Natures everich power and fors,
To store for Winteres derk and devyant course;
So push and pulle to twiste the DNA,
Thorough foule urea mark the embryoes way,
Lerne how to move, to stoppe, to dreame and thinke
Cast doubt into the wateres there to sinke.
Seke out the mysterie of feldes and fens
Thorough mirroires, and the optick fibred lens.

But in the serche for physickes sacred lore,
Beware the spirit of the dinosaur,
Who, suivant by the old Marsupial hounde,
Still ghostlie treads this hallowed earthlie grounde.
Beware, yonge soules, wherever ye may goe,
Of thinges which alchemie does not yet knowe!

Ode to Auterm

Season of lists and new achievement tests,
Prologue to weeks of joyless tedium,
Time to deliberate and digest
The acid of the new curriculum,
To bend with burdens the old teachers' knees
And fill with binders every classroom store,
To paint once more the rural studies sheds,
To set in place the targets laid by law,
And still more, to find the INSET speaker's fees,
And prune again the dangerous playground trees
Before, like rolls, they fall on unsuspecting heads.

Where are the seeds that fell from ERA?
Think not of them, they died in some distress;
Around the academic fields they lay,
Blown by the cruel winds of LMS
Ay, in a wailful cry they all return,
Half reaped concepts nobly borne aloft,
Sown in the heady scent of summer flowers
(Dulled by the thought of what each bloom may earn)
Dreamt in the inns where hopeful ale is quaffed —
Cooled in the dark of some accountant's loft
Dead, like the new term's non existent powers.

"Than longen folk to goon on pilgrimages"
(the NUT Conferences at Scarborough 1990/91)

The Scarborough Tales ... a prologue

Whan Aprill doth with payments verye smal
Save techeres ones agayn from fiscal thral,
And hedes of scoles receyve withoute compleynte
The annual parameter of constreynte,
Than longen folk to gather and unite
Wher eche may tell the storie of hir plight;
And so fro every toun and shyres ende
To Scarborough the wery pilgrimes wende
To talke of testynge, tyme and werynesse,
And joigne in wordes of ever mounting stresse.
Some carry tales of candels brent at night
To keep hir fadynge manuscriptes in syghte,
Whyles otheres found redundant, fortunes fooles
Bewepe the local management of scoles —
Which find hir qualitie of servyse streyned
By fundes dyverted to the graunt maynteyned —
Thus stirred by Easteres optimistic breeze
They leve fro Croydon, Hackney and Kirklees
To seke some common sense in Yorkshyres eyr
And greetinges from his worship Scarborough's mayor,
Who hostes this confeyrence since tyme long gon —
And there too I must flye, and so anon ...

The Scarborough Tales

Bifil it on the evening as I lay
Withinne a taverne fit for teacheres pay,
A messager cam in with baudy shoute:
'Bewar, ther is a rumble set aboute!
Olde Kenneth Clarke, that sours of light and joye
Is heer to test his strengthe with MacAvoy!'
Oure hooste aroos with twynklynge eyen and speke,
'Yong man, they brain is trewely made of cake!
The scoundrel onely talkes at armes lengthe,
For combat swich as this he hath nat strengthe.
Oure hooste thenne served us everichoon vittaile
and glasses plenitent with Yorkshyre ale,
Thenne welcomed were folk fro neer and far,
And blessed he the confeyrence atte the Spa.
'Tomorwe when ye tak your sobre place,
Remember ye are ther by Goddes Grace.'

Nexte morne when the busynesse bigan
The lord mayre greted everich meyde and man
Thogh some whose carages coude find no place
Were lesse impressed by his courtley grace
(For whyle theyre horseless cartes were layde in lyne
They were accorded with a parkynge fyne.)
But soone was cast asyde this dyscontente
By wordes from the comynge presydente.

Feyre Anne Moran, a meyden from the Tyne
Swift broghte the parlous delegates in line
She speke with untolde plesaunce and delyte
Of her receite of presydential myght
She tolde a tale of witte and comick fors
The clerke who tryed to shoe the rennynge hors
But fast she moved awaye from simple jestes
And reysed the spectre foul of Clarkes testes
Sayth she 'This nyghte mare is no mythic masque
But part of everich teacheres daylye taske'.
Hir wordes stirred angre even in the meke
And countlesse were the folke who wished to speke,
Til fynalie the confeyrence agrede
That techinge and not testynge was the nede
And so to all assembled, mayre and gestes
They seyde 'We will not handle Clarkes testes.'

Lyke sonne light rysinge on the Eyster daye
Bold MacAvoy spake forth on teacheres pay
For thogh some busynesse was not yet ended,
The ancient standynge orders were suspended
To stresse the nede for further frayes and fightes
To proteste at denyall of theyre rites

Thenne blew the berded Horne a battel crye
And clept old Clarkes policyes a lye
And made compleynte of techeres justice rough
And shouted out ful loud "Enough! Enough!"

Upon the tyde of April fooles morne
Some delegates appeyred a litel worne
A ceilidh helde upon the Sonnedaye nyghte
Hadde sapped some of strengthe for the fyghte
Yet nonethelesse the issue of poll tax
Renewed the fors of bittre felte attackes
But more intenselye felte upon the daye
Was how to fighte future testynge fraye
Wolde there be ample fondes to sustayne
A lengthye and a troublesome campayne?

And so they parled al wekes end and mor
Whyle outsyde on the wyndswepte Scarborough shore
I spyed a figure cloaked in clerick dresse
Who mumbled as he paddled in dystresse
'Go back ye waves, retrete ye salty pestes,
I will not move until I have my testes.'

Full soon the mystes fell downe upon the sande
The Northern watres rose and then, anon,
The sonne went down throughoute thys troubled lande
And the techers eek the clerick al were gon.

Strange Meeting

November is the strangest month
Upon the open Scarborough shores,
Where many an icy Baltic front
Meets drizzle from the Yorkshire moors,
Where late upon a moonlit night
As mist rolled off the Northern Sea,
The NUT arrived in might
To plan its campaign strategy.

Executives with leather cases
Booked in The Esplanade, The Royal,
While others, tired, with chalky faces,
Found humbler refuge from their toil.

The night found groups of angry talkers
Repeating Old Man Moser's words
As round the bay, ascetic walkers
Communed with shrieking coastal birds.

Some, like the seagulls, cried for battle,
Careering round the castle keep,
But most were calm like tired cattle,
Returned to bed and went to sleep,
Where dreams of Houghton warmed each member
Though cruel winds swept round the bay,
Where all year round, not just November,
Erosion means much more than pay.
But in those dreams appeared a vision,
A frightful form in darkest blue
Which spake with creepy cold derision:
'Beware of Kenneth Number Two'.

The dawn saw constitutions worsen,
Frail appetities were clearly shaken:
And conference makes a ready person?
Scrambled eggs and words of Bacon . . .
Until they met with great emotion,
Forgetting late committee tiffs,
And images of pay erosion
Conjoined with metaphoric cliffs.

Down at the Futurist Apollo
They found a still-locked conference door,
And rhetoric grew faintly hollow
Beneath the rising tidal roar.

Within the hall the speakers waited,
Timorous tongues began to cloy,
Till silence fell and, elevated,
Appeared the form of McAvoy.
(Eliot said that Emerson
Had bound the human mystery
Into the shadow of a man —
And called that image History.
But he had never had the joy
To see the shining laser
Of sparkling horn-rimmed McAvoy
In double breasted blazer).

But McAvoy chose not to speak,
And gave the floor its head.
Though movements from his great physique Could strike a motion dead.

Quite soon the hall became electric
With fevered shouting high and low,
With eager, heartfelt dialectic
From boxing rules to Maginot.
Flat rate! Percentage! Higher Status!
Immediate action! No more talk!
Drove the conference to hiatus
The ancient state of dove and hawk.

A militant, with agitation,
Declaimed at length upon his feet,
Until restrained, to loud ovation,
He settled in his proper seat.

The final vote, to hold back action,
Came with a unifying cheer
And delegates from every faction,
Gave government until next year,
But made a New Year's resolution
And minuted a final thought,
To take the only real solution
That Scarborough was the last resort.

Outside the hall they thronged, excited
As breakers thundered in the dark,
Gods and pedagogues united . . .
An augury for Kenneth Clarke.

Wir Lügen und Betrügen

The Plowden fields are scattered
With dry infertile sand,
For they are fed and poisoned
By Clarkey's flighty hand:
He fills the teleprinter
With hyperbolic strain,
Then like a hunted sprinter
He totters off again.
All the lies around us
Are sent to give good cheer
To those who tote the casting vote
In this election year.

He is the undertaker
For schools both near and far,
The friendly moneymaker
For England's new bourgeois.
The governors obey him
By him their schools are fed,
Regardless of the children
And protests from the Head.
All the latest charters
Are writ in deepest blue,
To boost the polls with Tory souls
In nineteen ninety two.

The testing and the streaming,
The economic stress,
The academic creaming,
The bureaucratic mess:
Mere words are insufficient
To voice our grateful praise,
For we are ineffecient
And tremble at his gaze.
All his wondrous statements,
His rousing chanticleer!
Oh, who could fail to trust his tale
In this election year.

Whining to School

Winter's Tale

When plaster falls from classroom walls
And woodwork teachers bite their nails,
And classes meet in gyms and halls
When frozen funding tells its tales;
Then local managed schools must wait
Till when? Till Whit or some time near
The start of the financial year.

When classes reach the forty mark,
And teachers lose the listening art
When games are held in public parks,
Then children will begin to part
Unto those schools where good intent
Is bolstered by fifteen per cent.
From whom? From artful Clarke, there is no doubt,
The champion of the opted out.

When all around the heating fails
And coughing drowns the teacher's word,
And pennies raised from jumble sales
Are counted up and then transferred
Into a fund for warmth and light
To keep them through the winter night,
While gales do blow from east to west
And cunning Ken doth cream the best.

Morning Worship

Mrs Dover, in her Rover
Leaves at seven on the dot,
Looks the empty building over,
Puts the cleaners on the spot.
Stills the early morning jokers
With her managerial style,
Warns the furtive classroom smokers,
Casts a cold headteacher's smile

Then appear the cleanly shaven,
Senior teachers one, two, three,
Fresh from their suburban haven,
Cups of cold unfinished tea.
Round the polished boardroom table
Each conceals a worried tale,
Like the monkeys in the fable,
Sifting through the morning mail.

In tray, out tray, forward planning,
problems as yet undefined,
Buildings, finance, fuel and manning
Strain the anxious corporate mind.
None too soon they hear the purring,
Of an ageing, well kept car,
Enter, constant Mrs Wareing,
Guardian angel, Registrar.

Now the horde of common teachers
Leave their frail domestic forts;
Noble masks on crumbled features,
Hiding less than Christian thoughts.
All at last are thronged together,
At the silent stroke of nine,
First years ruffled by the weather,
Sullen fifth years strewn in line.

Tutors scan the congregation,
Check some mental progress chart,
Feeling fear and fibrillation
In the old collegiate heart.
Thus with little satisfaction,
Morning worship plays its part
Kicks the workforce into action,
Stumbling from a staggered start.

Il faut cultiver notre jardin

I must go down to the garden again
To cut back my neighbour's pine,
Full knowing the growth that's between us
Is legally his and not mine;
But this is a trifling nuisance
Compared to the term that's ahead,
With all of the tests and assessments
Entwined in its overgrown bed.

I must go back to assessment again,
To tasks that September supplies,
Forget about Rousseau and Reason
And clarity writ in the skies;
For there in the soils of the season
Exists an insidious seed
Whose growth threatens horrible treason
The plague of the Binderweed.*

I must return to the classroom again,
And dig out the summer's remains,
I must check the visits of creatures
Who eat into delicate brains.
I must gather fruit in the garden again
 To fill the big pie in the sky,
And all that I need is a paper and pencil
To write the ridiculous lie.

* The National Curriculum Binder — a self-producing cell with
many off-shoots of ridiculous proportion.

Victor Ludorum

Mr Victor rises early
Splendrous in his summer shirt,
Braves the breakfast hurly burly,
Sparkling, bright and extrovert.

Driving off with expectation
Mr Victor wears a smile
Sighing with anticipation
"Triple jump, and first year mile. "

In the staff room all assemble,
Dressed in sporty rigmarole,
Mr Victor starts to tremble,
Spies his bulging pigeon hole....

Profiles, many days completed,
Filtered back for emendation!
Comments altered, marks deleted,
Fill his soul with trepidation.

Gone the dream, the day of leisure,
Gone the thoughts of summer skies,
Gone the joys of sporting pleasure,
Cheerful shouts and eager cries.

On the field a strange procession
Bares its unprofessional knees,
Naughty boys with indiscretion
Smoke and swear behind the trees.

Glorious sunshine warms the meeting,
Relay races reach their peak
Palpitations, overheating
Pump the noise to fevered shriek.

Prizes, trophies, medals, speeches,
Cheers, applause from tired souls,
Clouds appear from Western reaches,
Warning summer thunder rolls.

Cooling rain descends, resplendent,
Children leave the littered park
Mr Victor sits, attendant,
Writing profiles in the dark.

Curricular Warfare

Waking to the stagnant boredom
Of another teaching day,
Thoughts of Owen, Brooke and Auden
Fill the clouds of moning grey,
Poignant chatter of the children
Turns to noise of shot and shell,
Batteries of legislation
Battle with the morning bell.

Fast we leave the morning meeting
Wary of the head's last joke,
In the yard the rain is beating
Careless of the battle smoke.
Marching into Christian worship
Searching for a common truth,
Striving for a point of reason,
Tired of teaching restless youth.

Ploughing over moonlike craters,
Hopeless targets far away,
Set by clumsy legislators
In the orders of the day
Down the corridors of darkness
Caught in throngs of thundering feet,
Jostled by unfriendly elbows
Till the whistle bids retreat.

Streaming

Confluence makes a powerful tide
As Bacon might have said,
A force to sweep all cares aside
If given half its head.

Water holds a mystic thrust
As Archimedes wrote,
A bold primeval upward thrust
That keeps the fleet afloat.

The waves combine with grace divine
And never change their route,
A truth that served to undermine
Unfortunate Canute.

The Lord alone can part the seas
To let his people go,
And physicists confirm the risks
Of splitting H_2O.

Let those who dream divisive schemes
Reflect on their bidet...
Remembering that a rolling stream
Bears all its sons away.

When Mrs Kelly Stoops

Soft and kindly Mrs Kelly
Wears her hair in golden tresses,
Speaks at length of Keats and Shelley,
Hints at opiate excesses.

Seldom takes a hard position,
Always sounding sympathetic,
Makes no moral supposition,
Labels them as young, prophetic.

Students see a kindred spirit,
Praise her for her liberal view —
Puzzle at her frequent visits
To the stock room or the loo.

Is this soul a frail descendant
Of the dead Romantic strain?
Does her quiet smile resplendant
Hold the key to Wordsworth's brain?

Others sadder, wiser, older,
Criticise her melancholy,
Make a judgement wiser, bolder —
Talk of decadence and folly.

Softly, kindly, Mrs Kelly
Whispers faintly scented breath:
"Wordsworth, Byron, Keats and Shelley,
Nature, Passion, Birth and Death."

Now beneath her measured paces
Old iambic drums begin.
Keats and Shelley, Mrs Kelly,
Laudanum and Gordon's gin.

Reprographica

In the rustic room of reading
Students pause in meditation,
Hear the noise of paper feeding
In the throes of duplication.

Hush, the sound of whispered voices:
'Back to back' and 'small reduction',
Conscientious, Ron rejoices
In his skills of reproduction.

Quietly he hums the lyrics
Of some distant thirties tune,
Duplicating metaphysics
Needed for the afternoon.

Clip of scissors, Tippex pasting,
Scentless Pritt in applicator,
Quiet joys that bear no wasting,
Bliss of Ron, the duplicator.

Invigilation
(Lines written Upon Intimations of Eternity)

The hall is hushed, the curtains drawn
Upon some other worldly scene,
Outside, the fresh cut tennis lawn
Displays a cruel and tempting green.

A hundred urgent thoughts are burned
Upon the cold, demanding page,
A hundred bodies oddly turned
To disregard the silent stage.

Invigilation, summer's solace,
Deliverer from strain and stress,
Gives little warning, hint or promise
Of solitary loneliness.

Three hours to stroll between the seating,
To amble slow and serpentine,
To seek the abstract thoughts of cheating,
The crib, the note, the scribbled line.

No haven now for Attic drama,
The props, the costumes and the lights —
The enigmatic bits of armour
Are evidence of other nights.

And stands the clock still at eleven?
That, surely, was an hour ago,
When joy of joys, what bliss, what heaven!
A fit of sneezing stole the show.

The clock stands still for one more hour,
Then clicks a minute going by,
One student coughs with cosmic power,
Another breathes a tragic sigh.

Oh, free me from this sad depression,
release my numbed and aching brain,
Relieve me for the final session...
And give me back my class again!

Developing Myfanwy

Freewheeling down a one in five
At devastating speed,
How marvellous to be alive
On her velocipede!
Negotiating hairpin bends,
Identifying fears,
Translating unexpected ends
To analytic gears.
Enhancing her efficiency
At unexpected gradients,
Implementing quality
With reverential radiance.
So marvellous to be alive,
Professionally superior,
Performing up a one in five
To match her own criteria.
Freewheeling down a one in four,
Her heart begins to beat,
The friendly wind begins to roar
Its whispers of defeat.
Determination thrills her thighs,
Her catsuit from St. Michael,
'Such joy, such bliss,' Myfanwy sighs,
'My first appraisal cycle!'

An Educational Exchange
(after Maastricht)

Wild apocalyptic horses
Beat upon the soaking plage,
Thunderous Atlantic forces
Sweep across the Côte Sauvage.
Lightning from the Callac mountains
Lays the battered coastline bare,
Travellers forge through streams and fountains
Down from Brest to St Nazaire.
In the forest thunder crashes,
Shadows cast a sombre hue,
Boreas stirs the sodden ashes
Floating in a barbeque.

Suddenly the weather changes,
Silence falls on field and copse,
From coast to Pyrranean ranges
Tempesta violenta stops.
Soon the clearings fill with vapours,
Far away a church bell rings —
A single damp cicada capers,
Sly mosquitos spread their wings.

Cars arrive, all GB plated,
Roofracked Ford and Peugeot,
Drivers tired and tyres deflated
Trundle to the camp below.
Sunlight smiles upon the meeting,
Brightens up the Euroscene;
Euroteachers Eurogreeting
In their tents of red and green.

Guten Tag. Bonjour. Good morning.
Ich bin Lehrer. Je suis prof.
Grussgott. Hi there! *Buena sera.*
For six weeks you have it off?
Dice graze pour cette journée:
Cacciucco, fleur de chou.
Bombalone, Veuve de Vernay...
Viva nineteen ninety two!

Summer's Lease

Home Thoughts From Abroad

The air is fresh, the sky is clear,
The morning sunlight warms the day,
A thousand teachers commandeer
The fast lane of the motorway.

Out of cities, through the shires,
Tense and tired and overwrought,
Threadbare nerves on threadbare tyres,
Driving to the channel port.

Far behind the hopeless targets,
Early briefing, registration,
Fragile economic markets
Built on careless legislation.

Teachers and their nervous spouses
Set to face the ferry parking,
Ponder vaguely on their houses,
Strewn with piles of summer marking.

Far from lakeland, far from Avon,
Into dark and cold Boulogne,
Dreaming of a canvas haven
In the deep and green Dordogne.

Working parties, stale committees,
Minutes, marks and endless lists,
Disappear as magic cities
Rise up from the Gallic mists.

Bonjour madame. Bonjour patron.
Veux-tu quelque chose à boire?
Can I have a something citron?
(Safer with a café noir.)

Safer still within the campsite,
Shrill cicadas, scented pines,
Forest shadows in the lamplight
Settle peace on troubled minds.

Joy of morning, wildest wishes!
Breakfast in the whispering trees,
Watching colleagues washing dishes,
Baring unprofessional knees.

Here, a head in desert sandals,
Careless of the gross imprudence,
Paves the way for future scandals,
Dancing with the Spanish students.

There, a government inspector
Quotes at length from Rabelais,
Drowning like some ruddy spectre
In a sea of Beaujolais.

Noisily in wild aquatics,
Senior teachers, MPGs,
Join in childish acrobatics,
Laughter rippling on the breeze.

All too soon the dream is over,
Maps are spread in concentration,
Some say Portsmouth, some say Dover,
Some just stare in trepidation.

Night time falls and conversation
Bubbles round the barbecue,
Boiling up to Education,
Like a warmed-up verbal stew.

"I'm in charge of forward planning,
LMS and equal ops."
"I'm responsible for manning,
Playtime, crisps and lollipops."

Egocentric, brusque expressions
Shouted over dying embers,
Resurrect the wild obsessions
Borne by many sad Septembers.

All at once the Mistral settles,
Calming troubled mental seas,
Moonlight turns to silver metal,
Logic stills the fickle breeze.

From the waves a voice of reason
Penetrates their fuddled heads:
"No more talk of classroom treason,
Get you to your canvas beds!"

On the ferry in the morning,
Staring down into the foam,
Tired minds recall the warning.
What will wait them all at home?

Was it real, that stern upbraiding,
From the eerie moonlit brine?
Was it just a mental fading
Brought upon by too much wine?

Grip the handrail sturdy teachers,
Shun the metaphoric stern!
Storm those academic beaches . . .
Twelve more weeks to end of term.

Fin de Semestre

"Will Mrs Kelly call reception..."
(How far away the airport scene)
Her glass attracts the sun's reflection
Beside the sparkling, blue piscine.

Within its glacial microcosm
She swirls the icy cocktail treats
And clutches to her joyful bosom
Words of Shelley, works of Keats.

So far away invigilation,
So far the ache of unmarked papers,
The futile, vain investigation
To trace the source of classroom vapours.

A tiny bell across the borders
Invites the dreamers in to dine,
To where le garçon takes the orders,
To where le mâitre will pour the wine.

So far away the class of forty,
The forty dog-eared dirty books,
The faces foul, the faces haughty,
The faces filled with vacant looks.

All this behind her for a season,
The tired teacher takes her place,
And summer languor calms her reason
Until she spies a well known face...

"Oh, Mrs Kelly. Quel miracle!
I wasn't sure, could this be you?
So calm away from school's debacle.
May we join...excusons-nous"

"Tis ever thus, sighs Mrs. Kelly,
Her rising hopes returned to bed,
What vile touristic Machiavelli
Could book me in here with the head?"

Beside him sits his wife a teacher
Her visage pained and strained, unwell
"How nice to see you Mr Meacher,
How nice to see you Annabel!"

Poor Annabel, a mask tormented,
As if she dwells on dreadful crimes,
Her voice comes toneless, low, demented:
"I think we live in testing times."

The testing meal is long in pauses
From *crudités* to *glace vanille*,
When, *horreur*, in between the courses,
She feels a hand upon her knee.

In haste she leaves the scene of scandal,
And disappears into the trees,
Where, twisting on a broken sandal,
An awesome image makes her freeze.

Appearing through the scented bushes
Bearing, Pan-like, laurel sticks,
A boy in bright Bermudas blushes
Young Browning of the lower sixth!

"O do not fear, my lovely mistress!
Long have I worshipped you afar.
I saw in wrath your aweful distress,
And nothing shall my vengeance bar.

O Mrs Kelly give permission,
Please let me be your honest knight,
Allow me but this one commission
To put your dreadful wrong to right."

Her spirit sinks and, falling, falling,
A voice inside cries *aidez-moi!*
While, all the forest creatures calling,
She drifts into a *film noir.*

That night she lies in trepidation
'Till reason tells her to forget
And blames the ludicrous sensation
Upon the lagging of the jet.

She washes quickly, combs her tresses,
(Not looking at the cold bidet)
Dabs on cologne and calmly dresses,
Va prendre le petit déjeuner.

The cold croissant is hard to swallow,
The coffee has a bitter taste,
A distant voice cries follow, follow,
And so she leaves the scene of waste.

She finds a bar down in the maze,
A reeded river flowing by,
Where, sipping absinthe in a haze,
She, oh so softly, starts to cry.

Into the reeds glides Mrs Kelly,
Her tresses woven in watery charms,
Ophelia to a long lost Shelley,
Till fingers pluck her naked arms.

"Oh, Mrs Kelly, what deception!"
She hears the screaming of a jet.
"Will Mrs Kelly call reception?"
Have I not left the airport yet?

"Will Mrs Kelly call reception?
The Air France flight departs at once!"
Oh, bliss! Oh, joy! Oh, soul's perfection!
And now, *les vacances, elles commençent.*

The Caped Crusader.

See how he stands in a scarlet cloak,
Woven from Woolworth's terry towelling,
Turning his back on the steamer's smoke,
Raising his head to the seagull's howling,
Calling his children away from the water,
Hardening his heart to the youngest tear,
Leading her home like a lamb to the slaughter,
Blind to her pain like a seaside Lear,
Heedless of laughter from brown leather locals,
Baring his legs like a baptist preacher,
What could he be in his tinted bi-focals?
Surely, he must be, of course... he's a teacher.

September Song

Darkness falls on summer gardens,
Lager chills in sunburnt hands,
Cold lasagne verdi hardens,
Hardy lovers leave the sands.

Children beg for extra money,
Change for ancient fruit machines,
Sunpeeled noses turn all runny,
Mixing chocolate and ice creams.

Night arrives upon the campsite,
Teachers force the last pint down,
Staring at the fading lamplight,
Wishing they were back in town.

All around the British Isles,
British teachers on the run,
Wearing weary teachers' smiles,
Wishing they were having fun.

In the caravans they caper,
Squeezing grease from sandy cloths,
Using last week's Sunday paper,
Killing flies and maiming moths.

Snug withing their hardboard boxes,
Pedagogic nightmares strain,
Children dream of fields and foxes,
Downward falls
                    the
                        autumn
                                    rain.

75

The Rime of the Ancient Janitor

It is an ancient janitor
And he stoppeth one of three.
The new appointed acting head,
The registrar and me.

His skinny hand plucks at my gown,
His fingers shake with fear,
I cast a senior teacher's frown:
"The first years wait me here!"

He draws me to his closet room
With scents of soap and tea,
He lights a bulb of sickly gloom
Then casts a stare at me.

Says he, "I've seen his like before,
He wears ambition's dress,
It happened in the days of yore
Before this L.M.S."

I was a porter kind and good,
The guardian of the keys,
A polisher of brass and wood
And seldom off my knees.

Until there came an acting head
To clear the school of dross.
He called the school at once and said
"My name is Albert Ross.

I've come to give the school a style
Of quality and choice!"
But some who listened paused a while,
Feared madness in his voice.

Each day as lesson bells rang out,
Out of his room ran he,
And, staring, he would wildly shout
Some new economy.

From dawn till dusk, no light would burn,
And in each murky class,
A host of fearful heads would turn
To see his shadow pass.

And when he took my keys away.
I felt the blow was final —
Until he posted me one day
Inside the boys' urinal.

"Stay here," he said, "and study this!"
And, pointing to the trough,
He showed me how to stop the hiss,
To turn the water off.

"Enough!" I cried, "I won't kow-tow!"
And gave my head a toss.
And, thus, 'twas with my angry bow
I felled young Albert Ross.

77

He cried, as lying nearly dead,
"Block up that leaking sink!
As long as I am acting head
The water's not to drink!"

So now I pass from school to school,
I have strange power of speech,
And when I see one act the fool,
To him my tale I teach."

What loud uproar bursts from the door?
The first years waiting there!
Then I must leave thee, janitor,
And lead them in a prayer!

... make good cheer

A Pitiless Winter's dream

It was Christmas night in the classroom,
As snow fell in silence outside
And the moon cast its light in a corner
Where Jill the probationer cried

Around her lay thirty-six boxes
Of unfinished angels and stars
While shadows like ghostly advisers
Peered in through the burglar-proof bars

An unfinished monster accused her
With threatening bottle-top eyes
For all round the floor lay the remnants
Of finished but uncooked mince pies

She gazed at the poetry corner
Once praised and admired by guests
It now bore the fearful inscription:
"My Standard Achievement Tests"

Sadly she turned to her labours
The national curriculum folder
When at once an amazing brightness
Came over her frail, burdened shoulder

She turned to behold a great brilliance.
A figure in scarlet and green
Stood smiling upon the sad picture,
Then spoke in a voice most serene.

"Fear not little weary probationer
For I have recorded your plight,
Your hard work and brave perseverance
Shall be well rewarded this night.

Each cloud has a silver lining
And that is a magical fact,
For I am the good teacher's fairy,
Missed out of the eighty-eight Act.

My role is to seek out good teachers
Whose lives have become one long chore
And give them a fixed E allowance
Which they will receive evermore

These teachers shall all be well favoured
Their classrooms shall no more be dark
And all of their documentation
Will henceforth be done by a clerk

And each shall be given new training
On how to provide happiness
For theirs will be heavenly classrooms
Without hierarchical stress

Their contracts will henceforth be altered
To limit the length of their day
And I shall be sole arbitrator
In all new discussions on pay."

Then down came a host of bright angels
Who carried her upward on high
Where Jill saw a marvellous fountain —
The one true cascade in the sky.

Jill looked in dismay at this latter
Then saw through a magical glass
The once Educational Secretary
Now standing in front of a class.

"That's right, Jill, your confident leader
Has finally altered his ways
He's been sent off to the chalk face,
To finish his last working days."

Then joy overwhelmed the young teacher,
Too much for her overworked head
She swooned and then fell ever downward
To wake in her own lonely bed

81

"Alas" she cried out upon waking
"Twas only a pitiless dream".
But there in her hand was a letter
In writing she'd not before seen.

You must not despair said the letter
There's only so much I can do
But when you are feeling downhearted
Think on to the year ninety-two.

Jill smiled and got dressed very quickly
(Twas nearly the end of the year)
Then went off to teach her young children
With seasonal feelings of cheer.

"Now children put down your assessments
And just give your atlas a glance
Today we will hear about Christmas
In Italy, Spain, Greece and France..."

Inspector! Inspector!
(A party game)

Spin a teacher all about,
Take him by the hair,
Throw the little creature out,
Drag him up the stair.
Dress him in inspector's clothes,
Mystify his brain,
Then blow pepper up his nose
And throw him down again!

The Governor's Christmas Party

The tavern stood upon the mountain
Surrounded by a sea of snow,
As moonlight cast a silver fountain
And winter ceased the river's flow.

Within its walls a clutch of governors
Gazed silent at the flickering coals
And looked in hope at weary travellers
Who came and went with icy souls.

As in a dream they turned together
To stare upon the rattling door
That they might greet some beast of heather
Which called across the frozen moor.

"When will he come?" one governor started,
"I don't believe he'll come at all."
Then winds did roar and peace departed
As he stepped in the waiting hall.

The stranger sought no invitation,
Assumed the headship of the group,
Then smiled with rosy veneration
Upon the battle-weary troop.

So you're the noble governing body,
Ken Clarke's administrative tool,
And you require my Christmas package
For Coldheart Comprehensive School?"

"O yes," they cried with greedy voices,
"We want to do it right away,"
"We want to maximise our choices,"
"We want to leave the LEA."

"We want to find a business contact"
"To pay for salaries and rent"
"And fund us through a single contract"
"That covers every chance event!"

The stranger smiled and nodded, knowing,
Then turned and cupped his frost-red ear,
For though the wind outside was blowing
A distant sound he seemed to hear.

As waking from some anaesthesia
He clapped his hands with festive cheer.
"Come landlord, break this morbid seizure
Bring tankards of your special beer."

"Excuse me," said a small accountant,
Who hadn't said a word all day,
"I feel it on us most incumbent,
To finish work before we play."

The stranger stared with eyes of thunder
And wind howled fiercely through the door
As burning coals were cast asunder
Around the troubled tavern floor.

"Perhaps one glass," the governor stuttered
"And quite right too!" the stranger scoffed
And so before a word was uttered
The ale was poured and raised and quaffed.

Quite soon the governors' eyes were twinkling
And laughter filled the merry room —
And none had but the slightest inkling
Why brightness shone where once was gloom.

They woke next day with satisfaction
Another jewel, another crown
And sped to revel in their action
At Coldheart School in Coldmoor town.

A special meeting raised the question
"This central funding still in doubt."
The caucus laughed at this suggestion-
"The deed is done, we've opted out!!!"

85

At this the body broke decorum
And furious voices bawled and cried,
Until wild shrieking called the quorum
Into the snowfilled yard outside.

A horsedrawn sleigh stood in the whiteness
And children laughed with Christmas joy,
Where, someone dressd in scarlet brightness
Gave presents to each girl and boy.

"And for your head," he shouted gaily
"there's funding for a full time clerk.
And for your games we give you, daily,
Free access to the public park.
And for your teachers some surprises,
We give to each and every one
Allowances of healthy sizes,
And ratios of ten to one,
And, oh, I see some governors fretting
About that night upon the moors.
Well I'm quite sure, and here I'm betting,
You didn't read the Santa Clause!"

"The Santa Clause?" one governor shouted,
"What clause is that? I'd like to know"
The stranger laughed, "Is my word doubted?
Then I will take my leave and go!"

Whence came this red faced desperado?
Nobody knows unto this day.
Some say he hailed from El Dorado...
But others whisper "LEA"
For when the winter snow is falling
And economic winds do blow,
And governors hear the market calling,
You're safer with your CEO.

Chester Advent

In a little coffee shop
Down on Eastgate Row,
I sit and cast a tired smile
Upon my term time beau.

No more picnics down the lane
In his cosy car.
No more huddling from the rain
In some little bar.

Patiently I tolerate
A patronising kiss.
"See you on the first day back?"
My heart begins to miss.

"Passion is a cruel knife..."
He must think I am bats.
He'll spend Christmas with his wife
While I sit doing SATs.

The Lollipop Man

The early snow fell fast on hills,
And winter greyness filled the skies,
As Northern winds brought bitter chills
And distant children's playground cries.

Down in the little valley school
A whistle blew the end of play,
And children, wary of the rule,
Stood still as if they meant to pray.

But then, again, the whistle blew
And to the classroom they returned
And made a very formal queue,
 To settle where a coal fire burned.

Around the room were Christmas trees
And cribs and stars of every kind,
Though hidden by these festive scenes
Lay scores and tests, not far behind . . .

And on the teacher's crowded desk,
Beneath the tinsel and the crepe,
No one could miss the form grotesque,
The cold assessment binder's shape.

But all the children raised their eyes
To hear their well-loved teacher's voice
Though what they heard were nervous sighs
And mumbled words, like "freedom, choice ".

"We have a visitor today,
He's here to have a word with you,"
And in he walked, a man of grey,
Dressed in a suit of darkest blue.

His skin was cracked, his eyes were holes,
And when he smiled his face was strained,
He uttered words like "falling rolls"
And "central fund" and "grant maintained".

He left them in bewilderment,
His icy footprints on the floor,
And when he'd gone an evil scent
Came drifting through the open door.

Their teacher bent her body double,
Her shoulders shook with helpless grief
"Is there no INSET for this trouble?
No kind adviserly relief?"

Just then the school door burst agape,
Caused every little heart to stop
For there appeared in plastic cape
The guardian of the lollipop.

"Don't cry poor Jean," he called her name
"And children put aside your fears.
Just trust in me, you know my fame
For drying pointless infant tears.

I'm blessed with many a magic power
To use when children are distraught,
And now it seems we've reached the hour,
To stop this Whitehall juggernaut!"

"Come follow me you harmless creatures,
We'll soon escape the Tragic Act,
This beast of monstrous, awful features,
Devoid of human sense or tact."

The children rose with eyes ecstatic,
Their teacher followed them with pride
Considered: is this move erratic?
Then joined them in the snow outside.

The old man's words became emphatic,
His wintry breath impatient now,
"Into the bus," he breathed, asthmatic,
"There's not much time to keep my vow."

And so amid the winter's cold
While time and education waited,
The minibus was turned to gold,
Was most mysteriously translated.

The golden carriage flew on high,
The children cheered as one,
And soon it mingled with the sky,
Glowed brightly, and was gone.

When morning came they searched around,
And wandered high and low,
But nowhere could the school be found,
Just ever thickening snow.

The locals tell this tale at Yule,
And none have any doubt
That this is logic's final school,
Completely opted out.

Vita Brevis

The holly in the little school
Will soon be boxed and put away
To serve some future frugal yule —
Recycled for another day.
In other halls, the festive walls
Are stripped down to the wood,
And tinsel, paper, silver balls
Are put away for good.

Let us go then...

The Love Song of L.M.S Chalkface

Let us go then you and I
When the curriculum is spread out against the sky,
Like a teacher anaesthetized upon the timetable.
Let us go through certain half completed sheets,
The pitiful defeats
Of restless nights spent threading themes
Through rigid stages, plans and schemes,
Sheets that quote Professor Cox,
Blind to any paradox,
To lead you to an overwhelming question . . .
Oh, do not ask 'what concept is it?'
Simply let them make a visit.

In the rooms the children tap their feet,
Talking of life in Ramsey Street.

And indeed there will be time
For the tired eyes to scan the programmed sheet,
There will be time
To prepare a sheet to summarize
The sheets you will complete,
There will be time to audit and debate,
And time to worry if your target's late,
Time for a hundred indecisions
And for a hundred last revisions.

In the rooms the teachers come and go
Talking of Baker's scenario.

I grow old, I grow old,
I will wait until my school is sold,
Oh, do not ask for whom it tolls
Or how to boost the falling rolls.

In the rooms Inspectors come and go
Talking of last week's video.
Chalkblind, I have seen them all,
The role-play games of bat and ball,
The subtle tricks of domination,

Economy of information,
Oh I have heard them,
Those who do not teach,
Whisper words of closure, each to each
And, in short, I was afraid.

In the room the talk of revised criteria,
Bubbles to thinly disguised hysteria.

Yes, I have told them all of Christian gods,
Disregarding sleepy nods,
And faces stretched by early morning satellite,
And eyes that say "There will be time
To play another war game yet,
To just insert one more cassette . . ."

In the rooms accountants play their games,
Talking about redundant teachers' names.

And all the time I wonder "do I care?"

A redundant teacher's note to the milkman

I won't need any milk today,
In fact I'll be quite far away
(In Athens, Rome or Cairo).

You see there's been a big mistake,
The sort that good computers make
(they've overpaid my Giro).

I know five thousand won't go far —
I've bought myself a little car
And hope to get to Zanzibar

(Forgive the leaky biro).